Nature

Karen Hosack

Heinemann Library
Chicago, Illinois

© 2005 Heinemann Library
a division of Reed Elsevier Inc.
Chicago, Illinois

Customer Service 888-454-2279
Visit our website at www.heinemannlibrary.com

Designed by Ron Kamen and Celia Floyd
Illustrations by Jo Brooker
Originated by Dot Gradations Ltd
Printed and bound in China by South China Printing Company

09 08 07 06 05
10 9 8 7 6 5 4 3 2 1

Library of Congress Cataloging-in-Publication Data
Hosack, Karen.
  Nature / Karen Hosack.
      v. cm. -- (How artists view)
  Includes index.
  Contents: How artists see nature -- Bold shapes -- Bright colors -- Patterns in nature -- Old and modern techniques -- Close-ups on nature -- Tree silhouettes -- Painting outside -- Palette painting -- Using nature in design -- Nature and illuminated letters -- The magic of painting -- Controlling nature.
  ISBN 1-4034-4854-X
  1. Nature in art--Juvenile literature. 2. Art--Juvenile literature. [1. Nature in art. 2. Art appreciation.] I. Title. II. Series.
  N7650.H67 2004
  704.9'43--dc22

                                      2003026363

Acknowledgments
The author and publisher are grateful to the following for permission to reproduce copyright material:

Andy Goldsworthy p. 7; Bridgeman Art Library pp. 8 (The National Gallery, London), 9 (Österreichische Galerie, Vienna), 12 (Graphische Sammlung Albertina, Vienna), 14 top (© ARS, NY and DACS 2004), 17 (Private Collection), 19 (The National Gallery, London), 22 (The Stapleton Collection), 24 (Lambeth Palace Library, UK), 29 (Luton Hoo, Bedfordshire, UK); Collection Christa Zetta, Galerie bei der Albertina, Vienna p. 23; Corbis pp. 16, 28 (Burstein Collection); Courtauld Institute Gallery p. 6 (© DACS 2004); Hamburger Kunsthalle p. 10 (© DACS 2004); National Gallery, London p. 18 (Gere Collection); Natural History Museum, London p. 14 bottom; New Line Productions, Inc. p. 27 (All rights reserved); Photo12.com p. 4 (ARJ Paris, Musée du Moyen Age); Science Photo Library p. 15 (Susumu Nishinaga); Sterling and Francine Clark Art Institute, Williamstown, Massachusetts p. 20; Tate London 2004 pp. 13 (© 1998 Kate Rothko Prizel & Christopher Rothko / DACS 2004), 26 (© ADAGP Paris and DACS, London 2004); Trip p. 5 (H. Rogers); Tudor Photography pp. 11 x 4, 21 x 3, 25 x 3.

Cover photograph (*Flowers* by Andy Warhol, 1964) reproduced with permission of AKG (© The Andy Warhol Foundation for the Visual Arts, Inc./DACS, London 2004).

Every effort has been made to contact copyright holders of any material reproduced in this book. Any omissions will be rectified in subsequent printings if notice is given to the publisher.

Some words are shown in bold, **like this.** You can find out what they mean by looking in the glossary.

Contents

How Artists See Nature

Many artists look at nature to give them ideas for their work. For centuries artists have enjoyed studying the beautiful colors and shapes of the plants and animals around them. This **tapestry** was made more than 500 years ago. It shows two people, animals, and some trees and plants.

Lady with Unicorn, late 1400s

The patterns made by the plants and flowers in the tapestry on page four look similar to those drawn on the hands of this woman. Her hands have been decorated with **henna.** Henna is a natural plant **dye** that is used to decorate skin during some Asian and Middle Eastern celebrations and festivals.

Bold Shapes

The Dunes of Prerow
by Alexei
Jawlensky, 1911

These sand dunes were first drawn in curved lines using black paint. The spaces between the lines create large, bold shapes. Each dune has been painted in unusual colors. The red and yellow tops of the dunes help separate them from the dark blue sky.

Andy Goldsworthy is an artist who loves making art from natural things. This **sculpture** was made near a rowan tree that dropped its leaves. He sorted the colors of the leaves and carefully placed them in these circle shapes. The black hole at the center of the sculpture is made by the leaves that surround it. He took a photograph of the leaves because they would soon be blown away by the wind!

Rowan leaves with a hole by Andy Goldsworthy, late 1900s

Bright Colors

Sunflowers are a popular choice with artists because they are bright and bold. The most famous paintings of sunflowers are by Vincent van Gogh. Can you see that he has signed his name on the vase? Van Gogh decorated the guest room in his house with sunflower paintings when his friend Gauguin came to stay.

Sunflowers by Vincent van Gogh, 1888

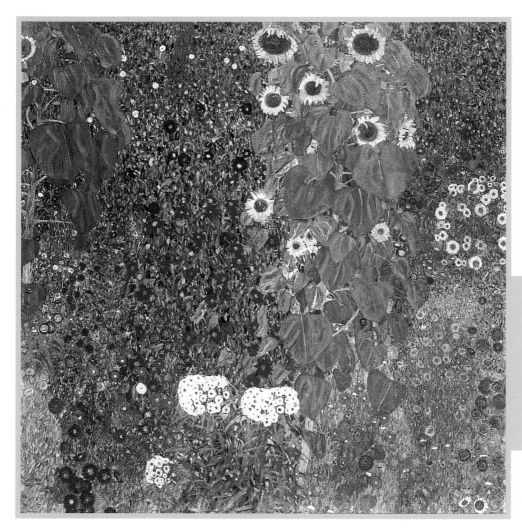

Garden with Sunflowers by Gustav Klimt, around 1905–1906

Sunflowers are the **focal point** in this painting. This means that our eyes are drawn toward them first. This is because they are larger than the other flowers, and bright yellow. A carpet of other flowers is painted in small colorful strokes. This gives the picture a hazy feeling, like a hot summer day.

Patterns in Nature

Paul Klee used the patterns of fish scales in this picture. The **focal point** is the large fish in the middle. All the other fish are swimming between pond plants and water squiggles. Can you see how Klee has not drawn every scale on the fish? With just a few marks he has made interesting patterns that give the impression of many scales.

The Goldfish by Paul Klee, 1925

Make your own sgrafitto picture

Paul Klee made his picture with oil paint and colored pencils, using a technique called **sgrafitto.** The following technique will give you a similar effect.

You will need:
- *a piece of thick paper or thin cardboard*
- *wax crayons*
- *poster paint*
- *a paint brush*
- *something pointed, for example a knitting needle*

Instructions:
1. Cover the paper or cardboard with multicolored scribbles of wax crayon.

2. Paint a thick layer of dark-colored poster paint all over the wax crayon background.

3. When the poster paint is completely dry, gently scratch a design using something pointed. The colors from the wax crayons will appear through the layer of dark paint!

4. You should now have your finished picture.

Old and Modern Techniques

Great Piece Of Turf
by Albrecht Dürer,
around 1503

This painting was made many years ago during a time called the **Renaissance.** During this period, people became interested in making paintings that looked very life-like. This study of plants is very detailed. The artist probably drew and painted it looking at a real piece of **turf.** This is known as working "from life."

This modern painting is very different. Rather than painting what could be seen from life, Mark Rothko painted how he felt about nature using only colors and shapes. We can only guess what he was trying to express when we look at this painting. He did not even help us by giving it a title! Perhaps he was painting the heat of the Sun on a sandy beach. The layers of yellow paint certainly glow like the Sun.

Untitled by Mark Rothko, around 1951–1952

Close-ups on Nature

Some artists look closely at flowers and plants to show how beautiful they are. Here, Georgia O'Keeffe shows the insides of some flower heads. When looking at her work you can imagine what a bee might see as it flies in for pollen.

Jimson Weed by Georgia O'Keeffe, 1936–1937

The picture on the left is a **botanical illustration** of an iris flower. It is a very detailed picture made by an artist. The picture helps the artist find out more about the iris. It is also helpful for other people who want to find out about the plant.

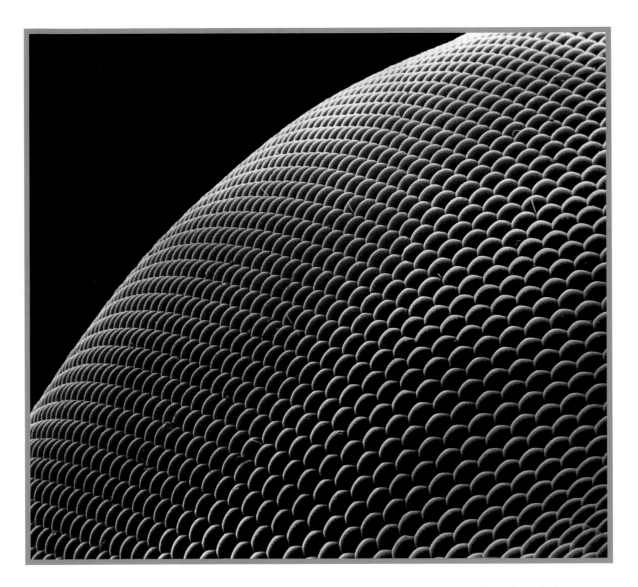

Photographers with special equipment can take highly
magnified pictures of things we usually cannot see.
This photograph looks like a complex pattern
designed by a clever artist. It is actually a close-up
picture of a fly's eye!

Tree Silhouettes

This tree was photographed either early in the morning at sunrise, or at dusk as the Sun was setting. Can you spot the Sun anywhere in the **background?** The front of the tree is in darkness, but the Sun lights it up from behind. This creates a dark shape called a **silhouette.**

Egon Schiele painted these three trees. The bright background and dark **foreground** in his painting also create silhouettes. The dark areas make us focus on the basic shapes of the trunks, branches, twigs, and leaves.

Autumn Trees by Egon Schiele, 1911

Painting Outside

This is a small **sketch** in oil paint. Simon Denis would have painted this sketch to help him with a larger picture back in his **studio.** Oil paints were not sold in tubes from a store when Simon Denis was alive. Artists at that time had to grind and mix their own fresh paints, which were difficult to carry around in large quantities.

A Torrent at Tivoli by Simon Denis, around 1789–1793

The Water-Lily Pond by Claude Monet, 1899

In the mid-1800s, oil paint started to be sold in tubes with screw-on caps. This made it easier for artists to paint big pictures outdoors. A group of artists called **Impressionists** began painting outside as much as possible. Claude Monet was a leading member of this group. This painting shows a pond in Monet's own garden. He painted the pond many times from different angles, in different seasons, and at different times of the day.

Palette Painting

The Artists' Palette with a Landscape by
Camille Pissarro, around 1877–1879

Camille Pissarro was also an
Impressionist painter. Here, he has
painted a **landscape** picture onto a
palette. Maybe Pissarro started playing
with the paint on his palette and it slowly
turned into a scene. Or perhaps he simply
ran out of canvases to paint on!

Did you know?
A palette
is a tool used
by artists to
mix paint on.

Paint your own palette landscape

You will need:

- *a piece of cardboard cut into the shape of a palette*
- *paint (poster paint, acrylic paint, or oil paint)*
- *paintbrushes*
- *a mixing palette*
- *water to wash your brushes (if you are painting with oil paint you will need white spirit instead)*
- *an old shirt to protect your clothes*

Instructions:

1. Find a scene through a window you would like to paint, then set up your painting equipment.

2. Make a quick line **sketch** of the main areas of your picture on your palette-shaped cardboard. Then use your real palette to mix colors that are as close as possible to the real colors you can see.

3. When you have mixed your paint, use different brush strokes to fill in the textures of clouds, leaves, grass, people, or buildings in the outline you painted on your palette-shaped cardboard. You should now have your finished palette landscape!

Using Nature in Design

Some designers copy the rich shapes and patterns found in nature. This wallpaper was designed by William Morris. By having patterns inspired by nature in a room, it brings the outdoors inside.

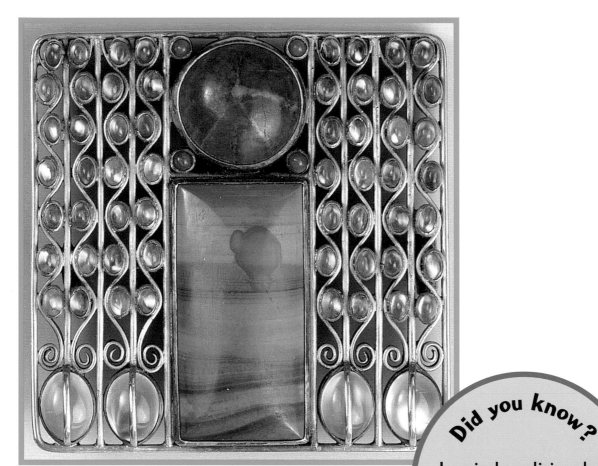

The design of this brooch uses the swirling shapes of plants. Natural materials like the blue **lapis lazuli,** mined in caves, and the pink-orange coral, from the seafloor, are set in silver. Other jewelry uses precious stones such as rubies, **amethysts,** diamonds, and sapphires. These stones are found in nature and take thousands of years to form.

23

Nature and Illuminated Letters

This letter was painted more than 800 years ago. It is covered with pictures of growing twisting plants, which wrap around the sides of the "B." Letters like these were designed to go at the beginning of important pieces of writing in books. We call them illuminated letters.

Decorate your own initials with things from nature

You will need:

- *a pencil*
- *a piece of paper*
- *paints or colored pencils*
- *some plants and flowers collected from your garden. Make sure you ask permission before digging anything up!*

Instructions:

1. Using your pencil, draw a large outline of the first letter of your first name. Next, draw a smaller outline of the first letter of your last name. You could put it inside the larger letter you have already drawn, or maybe it would look better by the side. You decide!

2. Next, use your pencil to decorate the letters with drawings of plants and flowers, using the plants and flowers from your garden to help you. When you have finished the pencil outline, color the design using your paints or colored pencils.

3. You should now have your own illuminated letters of your initials!

The Magic of Painting

Artists can make things happen in their work that could never happen in nature. This painting is like a dream. The **soft-focused** flowers look like they are floating and there are figures flying through the air.

Bouquet with Flying Lovers by Marc Chagall, 1934–1947

J.R.R. Tolkien created a character named Treebeard in his book, *The Lord of the Rings*. Treebeard is a huge walking, talking tree with branches for arms, twigs for fingers, and a face set into its trunk. This picture is taken from a movie made of the book. Treebeard was built by special effects artists. A massive tree structure was made in a workshop and **animated** like a puppet.

Controlling Nature

Claude Lorrain, known as Claude, used trees in his paintings like scenery for a play. Their dark shapes create a feeling of depth and break up the space in the pictures. Claude **sketched** the trees from real life and then used them later in his imaginary **landscapes.** He painted buildings in the same way. Many of Claude's paintings tell stories. This one tells an ancient Greek story.

Apollo and the Muses on Mount Helicon (Parnassus) by Claude Lorrain, 1680

People liked Claude's imaginary landscapes so much they wanted their own gardens to look the same way. The famous **landscape architect** Capability Brown was asked to design many gardens based on Claude's scenes. This one is at Luton Hoo, in Great Britain.

Glossary

amethyst   purple gemstone

animate   give life or movement to something

background   part of a picture that looks furthest away

botanical   to do with the study of plants

dye   substance used to color things

focal point   place in a picture to which the eyes are first drawn

foreground   part of a picture that looks the closest

henna   tropical plant that is used to produce a red-brown dye

illustration   drawing or picture in a book

Impressionist   one of a group of nineteenth-century artists who showed the effects of light in their pictures

landscape   picture of outdoor scenery

landscape architect   person who designs gardens

lapis lazuli   deep blue gemstone

palette   tool used by artists to mix paint on

Renaissance   period of European history between the 1300s and 1500s when there was a renewed interest in art

sculpture   piece of art made from a solid material

sgrafitto   art technique that involves scratching through a surface to reveal a different-colored layer underneath

silhouette   solid dark shape against a light background

sketch   rough drawing or painting

soft-focused   when something is blurred on purpose

studio   room where an artist works

tapestry   material with a woven or embroidered design, usually hung on a wall

turf   layer of soil covered with grass

More Books to Read

Heinemann Library's **How Artists Use** series:

- *Color*
- *Line and Tone*
- *Pattern and Texture*
- *Perspective*
- *Shape*

Heinemann Library's **The Life and Work of** series:

- *Alexander Calder*
- *Auguste Rodin*
- *Buonarroti Michelangelo*
- *Claude Monet*
- *Diego Rivera*
- *Edgar Degas*
- *Frederick Remington*
- *Georges Seurat*
- *Grandma Moses*
- *Henri Matisse*
- *Henry Moore*
- *Joseph Turner*
- *Leonardo da Vinci*
- *Mary Cassatt*
- *Paul Cezanne*
- *Paul Gauguin*
- *Paul Klee*
- *Pieter Brueghel*
- *Rembrandt van Rijn*
- *Vincent van Gogh*
- *Wassily Kandinsky*

Index